Published by Rock N' Roll Colouring Ltd® 2022

Artwork © 2022 Mark Wilkinson. Under license from Mark Wilkinson
except Iron Maiden 'Senjutsu' © Iron Maiden LLP. Iron Maiden
Under license to Global Merchandising Services Ltd
Judas Priest 'Painkiller' © Judas Priest
under license to Global Merchandising Services Ltd

Designer: Mark Leary at Asylumseventy7

All rights reserved. No portion of this book may be reproduced, stored in a retrieval system, or transmitted in any form or by any means, mechanical, electronic, photocopying, recording, or otherwise, without permission from the publisher.

First published in the UK by Rock N' Roll Colouring Ltd®
London
www.rocknrollcolouring.com

ISBN: 978 1 8381470 8 2

Printed in the UK by W&G Baird

The Official Mark Wilkinson Colouring Book
The creator of iconic designs for Marillion, Fish, Judas Priest, Iron Maiden & many more

I was obsessed with the album cover art I saw in the vinyl racks of music shops, the stamping grounds of a cultural revolution. It seemed to me to be the greatest contemporary art of my youth. To create record sleeves became my ambition. Learning how to draw is one thing though, to colour it all in is quite another!

You soon discover that there is no right or wrong way to create pictures. Every band is different but they all want the same thing in the end. A striking image! I was lucky to have worked with talented musicians whose LP covers provided a wealth of detail to colour in. I hope this book serves as a valuable resource and inspiration, to use as an initial template perhaps to express yourself further.
Good luck!

Mark Wilkinson

To see the original record covers featured in this book in their original, full colour glory
- please go to www.mark-wilkinson.co.uk/rnrcolouring

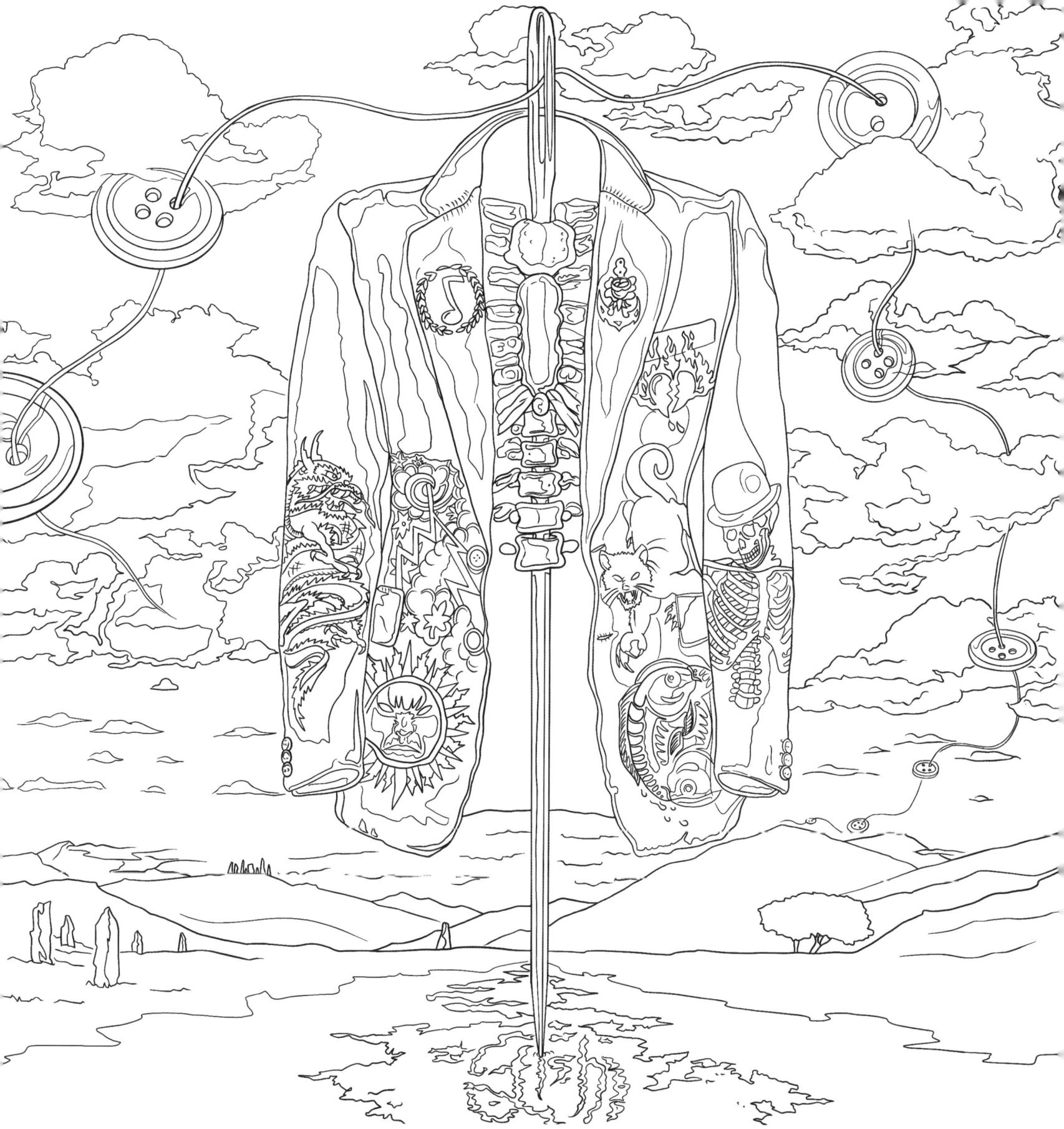

For your doodles

For your reference

1. Marillion 'Misplaced Childhood'
2. Marillion 'Best of Both Worlds'
3. Iron Maiden 'Senjutsu'
4. Fish 'Something In The Air'
5. Marillion 'He Knows You Know'
6. Marillion 'Script For A Jester's Tear'
7. Hawkwind 'Free Festivals'
8. Fish 'Suits'
9. Marillion 'Boy & Jester'
10. Justin Hawkins 'Snatching Defeat from Jaws of Victory'
11. Fish 'Tribal Logo'
12. Marillion 'Assassing'
13. Monsters of Rock 'AC/DC'
14. Marillion 'Market Square Heroes'
15. Marillion 'Lavender'
16. Crossbone Skully 'Evil World Machine'
17. Marillion 'Sugar Mice'
18. Fish 'Sunsets on Empire'
19. Masque Book Cover
20. Fish 'Vigil In A Wilderness of Mirrors'
21. Hawkwind 'Dave Brock'
22. Fish 'Yin Yang'
23. Marillion 'Kayleigh'
24. Judas Priest 'Painkiller'
25. Marillion 'Fugazi'
Doodle Page. Europe 'Prisoners Of Paradise'

To see the original record covers featured in this book in their original, full colour glory - please go to www.mark-wilkinson.co.uk/rnrcolouring

Also from Rock N' Roll Colouring

The Official Motorhead Colouring Book
The Official Judas Priest Colouring Book
The Official Megadeth Colouring Book
The Official Thin Lizzy Colouring Book
The Official Alice Cooper Colouring Book
The Official Iron Maiden Colouring Book
The Official Iron Maiden 'The Singles' Colouring Book
The Official Rodney Matthews Colouring Book

www.rocknrollcolouring.com